Most Popula

Caribbean Recipes

Quick & Easy

Essential West Indian Food Recipes from the Caribbean Islands

By

Grace Barrington-Shaw

More books by Grace Barrington-Shaw:

The information herein is offered for informational purposes solely, and is universal as so. The presentation of the information is without contract or any guarantee assurance.

The trademarks that are used are without any consent and the publication of the trademark is without permission or backing by trademark owner. All trademarks and brands within this book are for clarifying purposes only and are owned by the owners themselves, not affiliated with this document.

Disclaimer

All reasonable efforts have been made to provide accurate and error-free recipes within this book. These recipes are intended for use by persons possessing the appropriate technical skill, at their own discretion and risk. The author is not responsible or liable for any allergies, reactions, accidents or incidents of any kind that may arise as a result of cooking these recipes. It is advisable that you take full note of the ingredients before mixing and use substitutes where necessary, to fit your dietary requirements.

Table of Contents

Introduction

This book contains 16 of the most popular and tasty dishes in the Caribbean, simple and quick to cook, but mostly importantly, great to taste.

Whether you've been on holiday and caught the Caribbean vibe, or your heritage is from the West Indies like mine, I'm sure you'll agree that there is something about that warm, laid back attitude and sunshine feeling that draws you in. West Indian food embodies this feeling in every dish, warm, spicy and full of flavor.

Caribbean food is not one dimensional, most people are unaware of how adaptable this type of cuisine really is. Many dishes combine very well with non-Caribbean dishes while others are great on their own as snacks. These are just some of the reasons why Caribbean food is so popular for barbecues, picnics or eating on the go, as well as for a wholesome family meal.

I was born in Mandeville, Jamaica and spent most of my younger years there before working within the cooking industry at various locations around the Islands and eventually moving to the US, where I now live. As you can imagine I grew up watching my mom and family members in the kitchen, putting love and care into every dish they made. That sparked my passion for cooking this wonderful food, which is all about family, Sunday gatherings, and celebrations. Providing good meals for all family members and friends is key to Caribbean cooking and each recipe within this book reflects that, with a serving adequate for 4 – 6 people.

By the end of this book, you will be on your way to cooking like a West Indian...with passion, warmth and love. So bring back those childhood memories or impress your friends with an added Caribbean dish, now let's tour the islands and get cooking!

FREE Bonuses

We have 3 **FREE** bonus recipe ebooks for your enjoyment!

- **Cookie Cookbook** 2134 recipes
- **Cake Cookbook** 2444 recipes
- **Mac and Cheese Cookbook** 103 recipes

Simply visit: www.ffdrecipes.com to get your **FREE** recipe ebooks.

You will also receive free exclusive access to our World Recipes Club, giving you FREE best-selling book offers, discounts and recipe ideas, delivered to your inbox regularly.

Rice and Peas (Jamaica)

Although its origins are Jamaican, this is the quintessential dish throughout the Caribbean and is the basis of most good wholesome meals on the Islands.

Ingredients:

Rice (2 or 3 cupful's Long grain)
Black Eyed Peas or Red Kidney Beans (1/2 or ¼ Packet)
Water
Salt
Coconut Milk
Thyme
Onion

Method:

1) Start by soaking the peas or beans overnight in water.

2) In a pot of water, add salt and bring to boil.

3) Add thyme, coconut milk and onion. You should try to use fresh thyme if possible, for a more flavorsome taste.

4) Add the rice insuring water covers rice by ½ inch.

5) Cover rice with water in a pot and simmer.

6) Cook for 20 minutes until rice is cooked

7) Be ready to add additional water if needed so rice is nice and soft.

I use beans or peas according to who I am cooking for, you will establish your preference once you have experimented with both types.

Combine with:

Fish or meat dishes will taste perfect with rice and peas.

Dumplings Fried and Boiled (All Islands)

Dumplings make the perfect accompaniment for Caribbean and non-Caribbean dishes alike. Certainly, fried dumplings are very versatile, making a great snack and an absolute hit with kids.

Fried Dumplings

Ingredients:
3 cups of Self raising flour
2 teaspoons baking powder
1/2 cup butter
1 teaspoon salt (or sugar if a sweeter taste is preferred)
1/2 cup water
Frying Oil

Method:
1) Sieve flour into a bowl.

2) Add salt and baking powder, then stir in.

3) Cut the butter into pieces and add to the bowl.

4) Now knead the mixture as you would if you were kneading bread, using a massaging motion. Here we are trying to bind the mixture together.

5) Add water, just a little at a time.

6) You should now be finishing up with a large smooth ball.

7) Divide this large ball of mixture into smaller flatter shaped balls, similar to a donut shape.

8) Use your hands to mold the shape. The shape should measure 2 inches. They are now ready be fried.

9) Add a generous amount of oil into a frying pan with a low heat.

10) Fry the dumplings on both sides until they are a nice golden brown color. This usually takes around 5 minutes.

You can now serve your delicious fried dumplings, watch for the stampede from the kids - enjoy!

Boiled Dumplings

Ingredients (Same as fried dumplings)

Method:

Follow Steps 1-7 of the fried dumplings method.

   8) Boil the dumplings in a large pot over a medium heat for 15mins

   9) Drain the dumplings, then serve.

Combine with:

Eat your fried or boiled dumplings with a meat or fish dish or as a perfect snack by themselves.

Fried Plantain (All Islands)

Plantain is perfect to have as a side or snack and offers a sweet taste to a savory dish. This is one my absolute favorites and is an example of a dish that can accompany non-Caribbean dishes also. However please don't mistake these for bananas, they look very similar, but are larger with a tougher outer skin. When unripe they have a starchy taste until fully ripe, where they develop into a nice sweet taste.

Ingredients:
1or 2 Plantains
Oil

Method:

1) Cut the plantains open with a knife (it is difficult to peal them, you'll need to cut the ends of first. Then cut all the way along the ridges.

2) You can now peel the skin away in strips quite easily.

3) With the knife cut the plantain in half.

4) Slice the plantain into thin strips ready to fry.

5) Fry the plantain pieces with a decent amount of oil, on a low heat for around 15 minutes until nice and brown on both sides.

Combine with:
Plantains are fantastic with any Caribbean dish, but don't limit it, be creative and combine with any dish you see fit.

Saltfish Fritters (All Islands)

A very tasty twist on fish cakes, Saltfish Fritters are fried and are perfect as a snack or finger food.

Ingredients:
1/2lb of saltfish
3 cups plain flour
1 onion
1 pinch of salt
1 scotch bonnet pepper
1/2 teaspoon black pepper
1 clove garlic
2 cups water
Oil

Method:
1) Soak the saltfish in a bowl of water for half an hour.

2) Chop the garlic, pepper and onion into small pieces.

3) Once the fish has soaked, you can then pull the fish apart into small pieces.

4) Sieve the flour into a separate bowl.

5) Next into the flour add the garlic, pepper, onion and salt.

6) Slowly stir in some water until you achieve a sloppy consistency.

7) You are now ready to fry your fritters, add oil to the frying pan, around 1/2cm cm deep. Fry one side of the fritter for 10 minutes, then turn over and fry the other side for another 5minutes. Repeat for all the fritters.

Combine with:

These are great with bread or by themselves especially at parties!

Patties – Beef (Jamaica)

A favorite throughout the Caribbean, patties are a great snack and good alternative to a pie.

Ingredients:
plain flour
1/2 tub of frozen butter
500g minced beef
1 to 2 onions (finely chopped).
125ml Water
Salt
4 tablespoons breadcrumbs
1 teaspoon black pepper
1 to 2 Scotch bonnet (chopped)
2 to 3 teaspoons of curry powder
1 to 2 teaspoons turmeric
1 teaspoon paprika
1 teaspoon oil
1 stock cube
1 small piece of ginger (crushed)
3 garlic cloves (crushed)
2 tomatoes (chopped)
1 teaspoon dried thyme

Method:

Pastry

1) Sieve the flour into a bowl.

2) Next, add salt and turmeric to the bowl.

3) Grate the frozen butter and crumble the butter with your fingers.

4) Add the cold water.

5) Knead the mixture until you end up with a texture similar to bread.

Curried Mince

1) Heat the oil in a pot.

2) Add mince, onions, garlic, celery and ginger.

3) Once the mince becomes browned you can add the curry powder, scotch bonnet pepper, thyme, paprika, salt, black pepper.

4) Cook for a further 5 minutes.

5) Add tomatoes, cook for another 5 minutes until softened.

6) Add the breadcrumbs and stir in.

7) Then add water and stock cube, simmer for 30 minutes. This should create a thick stew, leave to cool.

8) Use a floured board, cut a piece of the pastry and roll flat.

9) Place a small saucer on the dough and cut around it creating a circle.

10) Pour approximately 1 to 2 teaspoons of curried mince mixture so less than half the circle is covered. Now fold the other half of the circle over and using a fork, press the joined edges together. This makes a half moon shape.

11) Using the fork, prick the patties twice which will allow the steam to release.

12) Cook in pre-heated oven for about 30 minutes at Gas mark 4 / 180 C.

The filling does not have to be beef, you can also make chicken and lamb or vegetable variations.

Combine with:

Eat with a rice or potato dish. Excellent when eaten by themselves.

Jerk Chicken (Jamaica)

Jerk Chicken is one of the most popular dishes for barbecues and outdoor functions. Jerk chicken dishes are full of succulent chicken with an added smoky flavor.

Ingredients

One whole 3lb chicken or 3lb of chicken breasts
6 sliced scotch bonnet peppers
3 Medium onions (finely chopped)
8 Cloves garlic, (finely chopped)
2 Tablespoon of thyme
2 Tablespoon ground allspice
2 Tablespoon sugar
2 Tablespoon salt
2 Tablespoon black pepper
2 Tablespoon of cinnamon
2 Tablespoon of nutmeg
2 Tablespoon of ginger
1 cup orange juice
1/2 cup olive oil
1 cup white vinegar
1/2 cup soy sauce
1 lime (for juice)

Method:

1) Chop the garlic, peppers and onions.

2) Next add all the ingredients, except the chicken into a blender, this makes the jerk sauce.

3) Now cut the chicken into 4 pieces.

4) Rub the sauce into the chicken, however leave some excess for dipping and basting later. The chicken now needs to be left to marinade overnight.

5) On the next day the chicken is ready to cook in the oven for 1 hour, 30 minutes each side.

6) While the chicken is cooking, baste with some of the remaining marinade.

7) Each quarter chicken needs to be cut into 5 or so smaller pieces. You will need something very sharp in order to cut the flesh and bone.

Combine with:

Serve with dumplings or festival, rice and peas and a side of salad. Don't forget the jerk sauce left over for dipping.

Jerk Pork (Jamaica)

Similar to the chicken version, within the West Indies, jerk pork is a popular dish for barbecues and outdoor functions.

Ingredients:

Same as jerk chicken except substitute chicken for pork
3 lb. of boneless pork loin

Method:

1) Chop the garlic, peppers and onions.

2) Next add all the ingredients, except the pork into a blender, this makes the jerk sauce.

3) Now cut the pork into smaller pieces, be sure to prick holes in the pork.

4) Rub the sauce into the pork, however leave some excess for dipping and basting later. The pork now needs to be left to marinade overnight.

5) On the next day the pork is ready to grill slowly. Ensure you regularly turn the pork until cooked.

6) While the pork is cooking, baste with some of the remaining marinade.

Combine with:

Dumplings or festival, rice and peas and a side of salad. Don't forget the jerk sauce left over for dipping.

Curry Goat (Jamaica)

A favorite throughout the Caribbean and across the world, curry goat is a great curry which is served at all West Indian parties and celebrations.

Ingredients:
1kg goat meat (remove bones)
3 tomatoes
1 Scotch bonnet
1 tablespoon salt
1/2 teaspoon dried thyme
1/2 teaspoon Allspice
1 teaspoon freshly ground black pepper
3 tablespoon curry powder
2 whole spring onions, sliced
1 onion, sliced
3 cloves of garlic, crushed
4 tablespoons oil
juice of 1 lime
1 tin of coconut milk

Method:

1) Use half a lime to cover the goat meat.

2) Place the meat in a substantial bowl, add the salt, pepper, thyme, allspice, curry powder, garlic spring onion, onion and Scotch bonnet. Marinate for 2 hours in the fridge.

3) Heat the oil in a frying pan with a medium-heat until very hot, add the meat to the pan only

4) Cook the meat until brown for around 5-6 minutes, then add all the seasoning mix and cook for a further 2 minutes.

5) Next add the tomatoes and cook until everything is combined for about 3 more minutes.

6) Add the coconut milk and around 2 more cups of water.

7) Reduce the heat to low and bring to the boil, then cover and cook until meat is tender. This will probably take a couple of hours.

8) Finally, Stir in the remaining lime juice.

Combine with:

Serve with rice and peas or plain white rice.

Stewed Fish (Jamaica)

This is a very popular way of cooking fish in the Caribbean, particularly for Good Friday.

Ingredients:

1 Whole Fish (cut evenly into pieces)
oil
salt
pepper
plain flour
onion (chopped)
thyme (chopped)
parsley (chopped
garlic (chopped finely)
coriander
sweet peppers
tomatoes
water

Method:

1) Use the coriander, thyme, parsley, onion, flour and garlic to season the fish. Marinate in the fridge for an hour.

2) Fry the fish in about 1 inch of oil until nicely brown and cooked.

3) Use a fresh frying pan to slowly cook sliced sweet peppers, some onions, garlic, three chopped tomatoes until they start to soften.

4) Next add 1/2pt of water, simmer for 15 minutes until the tomatoes have broken down.

5) Add 1 tablespoon of thick sundried tomato paste, season to taste with salt and black pepper.

6) Place the fish pieces into the mix and let it warm up and simmer for about 5 minutes.

Combine with:

Best served with rice for a great meal.

Stewed Chicken (Trinidad)

A sweet and tasty Caribbean dish that is so quick to make.

Ingredients:

1 small chicken
1 onion (chopped)
salt
black pepper
1 garlic (whole and chopped)
fresh coriander chopped
2 tomatoes
1 tablespoon dark soy
1 tablespoon brown sugar

Method:

1) Remove the skin from the chicken then cut into pieces, separate the wing, thigh and drumstick. Cut breast and back into 3-4 pieces.

2) Wash the chicken, then add to a bowl with the 2 chopped tomatoes and mix, leaving overnight in the fridge.

3) Measure 2 tablespoons oil in a frying pan and a heap tablespoon of brown sugar and place on a low heat until the sugar caramelizes.

4) Add the chicken to the frying pan, coating it in the brown sugar solution.

5) Let the chicken simmer until the sauce generated is bubbling, then cover the frying pan on a low heat.

6) Check the sauce level and add more water (cupful) if required. Leave for 15mins to cook, checking the taste regularly and adding salt, pepper or soy as you see fit.

7) Monitor the sauce level, if too much sauce, leave to cook down slightly. You should finish up with brown, sweet flavored chicken and sauce.

Combine with:

Rice and peas. Add plantain and sliced tomatoes for a little twist.

Cornmeal Porridge (Jamaica)

A really tasty porridge, which Jamaican's swear by. Cornmeal porridge is thought of as a great cleanser for your digestive system.

Ingredients:

1 cup of yellow cornmeal
Sugar (to taste)
1 cup of milk
4 cups of water
1/2 a teaspoon of salt
1/2 teaspoon of cinnamon
1/2 teaspoon of nutmeg
1/2 cup of sweetened condensed milk
1 teaspoon of vanilla

Method:

1) Use a bowl to place the cornmeal in and add 1 cup of water.

2) Mix the contents of the bowl.

3) Use a saucepan and mix one cup of milk and three cups of water bringing to the boil.

4) Once the water and milk has boiled lower the heat, stirring in the cornmeal mixture. Stir regularly and allow to simmer for 10 minutes.

5) Add the cinnamon, vanilla and condensed milk and stir in, allowing to simmer for another 4-5 minutes.

Combine with:

Fruits and oatmeal bread compliments this type of porridge very well.

Easter Bun (Jamaica)

A great traditional bun in Jamaica, not only reserved for Easter however.

Ingredients:

3½ cups flour
4 tablespoons baking powder
1 egg (beaten)
1½ cups sugar
1 tablespoon nutmeg
½ tablespoon cinnamon
½ tablespoon rose water
½ tablespoon anise extract
1 cup stout or beer
2 tablespoon butter (melted)
2 teaspoon vanilla
1 cup cherries
1 mixed peel & cup raisins
½ tablespoon ground allspice
pinch of salt

Method:

1) Use a bowl to mix baking powder, flour, salt, sugar and spices.

2) Add fruit, then mix.

3) Next add melted butter and beaten egg to the mixture, mix thoroughly until mixture is coarse.

4) Now add the stout or beer and mix thoroughly.

5) Pour the mixture into greased baking pans.

6) Bake for approx. 1¼ hours at 300 °F. If desired, press a few whole cherries into the top of each bun. Makes two meatloaf pans.

Combine with:

Perfect with cheese as a snack, however you can also treat this as a desert and serve with ice cream.

Festival (Jamaica)

A traditional Jamaican side, a type of dumpling slightly sweet and cornmeal flavored.

Ingredients:
1 1/2 cups flour
3 tablespoons sugar
1 teaspoon vanilla
3 tablespoons cornmeal
1 cup water
1/2 teaspoon salt
1 teaspoon baking powder

Method:

1) Sieve the flour into a bowl and add the baking powder, cornmeal, salt and sugar.

2) Add the teaspoon of vanilla to the cup of water.

3) Next you need to achieve a breadcrumb like texture by adding a small amount of water regularly while working the water in to the mixture with your fingertips. Keep adding small amounts of water until half of the cup has been added.

4) Having achieved the breadcrumb like texture you now need to achieve a firm dough, by continuing to add small amounts of water to the mixture. However, you should not need to use a whole cup of water for the process.

5) Once the dough is complete, cover the mixture and leave for 30 minutes.

6) Now divide the mixture into small portions, using your hands roll the portions into small sausage shapes.

7) Next cover the festival, in cornmeal and flour.

8) Add a decent amount of oil and deep fry until golden brown for 20 minutes.

Combine with:

Serve with any Caribbean dish. Especially Jerk and fish dishes which offsets the taste very nicely.

Ackee and Saltfish (Jamaica)

This is the national dish of Jamaica, Ackee is a Jamaican fruit which is very quick to cook.

Ingredients:

1 Tin of Ackee
1 teaspoon chicken stock powder
1 Onion roughly chopped
2 Fresh tomatoes
1 teaspoon Black Pepper
1 Knob of butter (optional)
1 Packet of salted cod fish.
1 Scotch bonnet (optional - for extra heat)

Method:

1) Use a saucepan, add water and the salted cod and boil.

2) Pour off the water and repeat 1-2 more times, depending on taste.

3) Next pour some more cold water onto fish and leave for 5, then drain.

4) Flake the fish into small pieces

5) Take a frying pan, add the oil, tomatoes, onion and scotch bonnet (optional) and fry until onions are soft.

6) Add the fish flakes along with the chicken stock mix in water adding the butter.

7) Cook for around 3-4 minutes.

8) Add the Ackee, and sprinkle with black pepper to season. Be sure to simmer on low heat for 3-5 minutes.

Your Ackee and saltfish is ready to serve.

Combine with:

I prefer to serve this with fried plantains and dumplings, either boiled or fried.

Pepper Pot (Guyana)

This is Guyana's national dish, popular at Christmas and celebrations this stewed meat dish is unbeatable.

Ingredients:

500 grams beef
3 Cow heels
1 scotch bonnet pepper
1 tablespoon vinegar
1 cup casareep
1 medium onion
1 spring thyme
2 cups water
3 cloves garlic
1 scallion
1/4 teaspoon salt
1 tablespoon soy sauce

Method:

1) Wash meat, then clean meat with vinegar.

2) Cut meat into small pieces. Season the meat with soy sauce, chopped onion, garlic, scallion, thyme and salt. Rub in ingredients well.

3) In a pan, add the cow heels with enough water to cover, bring to boil over medium heat. Simmer for 1 hour

4) Add all seasoning to the pan and cook for a further 2 hours. You should finish up with a nice thick sauce with tender meat.

Combine with:

Perfect with bread or rice.

Johnny Cake (Bahamas)

A tasty cornmeal cake with many different versions across the islands, however the Bahamian version tends to rely on less cornmeal.

Ingredients:

1 cup flour
1 egg (beaten)
5 tablespoon baking powder
3/4 cup cornmeal
3/4 tsp. salt
1 cup milk
1/3 cup sugar
2 tablespoon vegetable oil

Method:

1) Firstly, preheat oven to 350F.

2) In a bowl add the flour, baking powder, cornmeal, salt and sugar. Mix well.

3) Next add the egg, milk and oil to the mixture and again mix very well.

4) Pour the mixture into an 8 inch square pan.

5) Bake for 30 minutes, until the cake is brown on top.

Serve hot or cold with butter, honey or preserves.

Combine with:

Eat with honey, or simply butter.

Roti (Trinidad)

This is a popular bread to eat at breakfast for Trinidadians, but can be eaten with just about any meal

Ingredients:
4 cups all purpose flour
1 cup water
2 tablespoons baking powder
1 tablespoon vegetable oil, plus more for cooking roti
1 teaspoon salt

Method:
1) Start by using a mixing bowl to combine the flour, salt, baking powder to make the breads. Be sure to make a well in the center of the mixture.

2) Next mix the oil and water in a separate smaller bowl and add this mixture to the well.

3) Knead for around 5 minutes in order to make a dough. The dough should be smooth when complete.

4) Divide the dough into 6 balls, cover with a damp kitchen towel and leave for two hours.

5) Next, lightly flour a clean surface, then roll each ball of dough into flat, thin circle measuring about 9 inches in diameter. Be careful not to stack the breads, once you've finished rolling.

6) Heat a large griddle with high heat adding 2 teaspoons of vegetable oil.

7) Once the griddle is hot, you can add the bread dough, cooking for around 1 minute, you will then see brown spots forming. Turn the bread and cook the other side for 1 minute.

8) Once cooked, transfer to a plate and cover with a damp towel in order to keep the Roti warm as you complete the rest of the breads.

Combine with:

Compliments just about any meal, great with dips and soups.

Caribbean Tools & Utensils

Whilst preparing and cooking your Caribbean meals, you may want the assistance of correct utensils. The table below lists the utensils that will greatly help achieve the Caribbean dishes that you desire.

Utensil	Description	Use
Dutch Pot / Oven	A strong cast iron cooking pot with thick walls	Used for cooking meats, stews, soups and rice
Mortar and Pestle	Small ceramic or stainless steel bowl with blunt crushing instrument	For grinding and crushing herbs and spices into paste
Calabash Bowl	Large bowl made of hardwood	Used for serving
Wooden Spoon	Large bamboo spoon	Used for serving
Knife Set	A professional knife set with various sizes	Needed for slicing meat and vegetables
Caribbean Cookware Set	A complete set of dutch pot, skillet and sauce pan	For all food cooking

Visit the site below to see images of recommended utensils:

http://www.ffdpublishing.com/caribbean-tools-utensils/

Thank You

I hope you have enjoyed this book and by now have cooked some wonderful Caribbean dishes.

If you've enjoyed this book and have found that the recipes have helped you, can I ask if you could please spare a moment to leave a review.

Don't forget to expand on your newly gained cooking skills by deep diving into Jamaican recipes with my Jamaican food recipe cook book or mix your own great tasting Caribbean cocktails with 60 of the world's best cocktail recipes from the Caribbean, both available on Amazon:

Also, remember to visit www.ffdrecipes.com for your FREE bonus recipe ebooks and to get exclusive access to our World Recipes Club, which provides FREE book offers, discounts and recipe ideas!

Thank you.

Cooking Measurements & Conversions

Oven Temperature Conversions

Use the below table as a guide to establishing the correct temperatures when cooking, however please be aware that oven types, models and the location of your kitchen can have an influence on temperature also.

°F	°C	Gas Mark	Explanation
275°F	140°C	1	cool
300°F	150°C	2	
325°F	170°C	3	very moderate
350°F	180°C	4	moderate
375°F	190°C	5	
400°F	200°C	6	moderately hot
425°F	220°C	7	hot
450°F	230°C	8	
475°F	240°C	9	very hot

US to Metric Corresponding Measures

Metric	Imperial
3 teaspoons	1 tablespoon
1 tablespoon	1/16 cup
2 tablespoons	1/8 cup
2 tablespoons + 2 teaspoons	1/6 cup
4 tablespoons	1/4 cup
5 tablespoons + 1 teaspoon	1/3 cup
6 tablespoons	3/8 cup
8 tablespoons	1/2 cup
10 tablespoons + 2 teaspoons	2/3 cup
12 tablespoons	3/4 cup
16 tablespoons	1 cup
48 teaspoons	1 cup
8 fluid ounces (fl oz)	1 cup

1 pint	2 cups
1 quart	2 pints
1 quart	4 cups
1 gallon (gal)	4 quarts
1 cubic centimeter (cc)	1 milliliter (ml)
2.54 centimeters (cm)	1 inch (in)
1 pound (lb)	16 ounces (oz)

Liquid to Volume

Metric	Imperial
15ml	1 tbsp
55 ml	2 fl oz
75 ml	3 fl oz
150 ml	5 fl oz (¼ pint)
275 ml	10 fl oz (½ pint)
570 ml	1 pint
725 ml	1 ¼ pints
1 litre	1 ¾ pints
1.2 litres	2 pints
1.5 litres	2½ pints
2.25 litres	4 pints

Weight Conversion

Metric	Imperial
10 g	½ oz
20 g	¾ oz
25 g	1 oz
40 g	1½ oz
50 g	2 oz
60 g	2½ oz
75 g	3 oz
110 g	4 oz
125 g	4½ oz
150 g	5 oz
175 g	6 oz
200 g	7 oz
225 g	8 oz
250 g	9 oz
275 g	10 oz

350 g	12 oz
450 g	1 lb
700 g	1 lb 8 oz
900 g	2 lb
1.35 kg	3 lb

Cooking Abbreviations

Abbreviation	Description
Tsp	teaspoon
Tbsp	tablespoon
C	cup
Pt	pint
Qt	quart
Gal	gallon
Wt	weight
Oz	ounce
Lb	pound
G	gram
Kg	kilogram
Vol	volume

Ml	milliliter
L	liter
fl oz	fluid ounce

20759734R00029

Printed in Poland
by Amazon Fulfillment
Poland Sp. z o.o., Wrocław